Collecting Lost Coins

21 Days of Celebration with Young Life

Collecting Lost Coins

Scripture taken from the HOLY BIBLE, NEW INTERNATIONAL VERSION ®. Copyright © 1973, 1978, 1984 by International Bible Society. Used by permission of International Bible Society.

"NIV" and "NEW INTERNATIONAL VERSION" are trademarks registered in the United States Patent and Trademark office by International Bible Society.

Scripture taken from the NEW AMERICAN STANDARD BIBLE ®, Copyright 1960, 1962, 1963, 1968, 1971, 1972, 1973, 1975, 1977, 1995 by The Lockman Foundation. Used by permission.

Scripture taken from the KING JAMES VERSION.

Inquiries regarding permission for use of the material contained in this book should be addressed to:

> Young Life Communications
> P.O. Box 520
> Colorado Springs, CO 80901
> (719) 381-1800

Printed in the United States of America
ISBN 0-9770338-1-3

The stories in this book have been collected from a variety of sources, including articles, newsletters and letters from the President's Office. When necessary, without notation, the names have been changed to respect the privacy of our friends. Special thanks to Billy Doyle and Donna McKenzie for their contributions to Day 14 and Day 21, respectively. Scripture is taken from the New International Version of the Bible unless otherwise noted.

Table of Contents

Foreword .... by Denny Rydberg
Welcome to the Party.. 9

Celebrating the Search

Day One... 17
Day Two.. 21
Day Three 25
Day Four.. 31
Day Five 35
Day Six.. 39
Day Seven 43

Celebrating the Find

Day Eight 51
Day Nine.. 55
Day Ten.. 61
Day Eleven.. 65
Day Twelve 69
Day Thirteen 75
Day Fourteen 79

Celebrating the Shine

Day Fifteen.. 87
Day Sixteen 91
Day Seventeen 95
Day Eighteen 99
Day Nineteen.. 103
Day Twenty... 107
Day Twenty-one.. 111

Foreword

*Y*ou may be familiar with Richard Foster's best-selling book, *The Celebration of Discipline.* John Ortberg, pastor and author, has suggested someone write a second book, *The Discipline of Celebration!* In other words, we need to practice throwing parties and praising God! We agree with Ortberg in Young Life. We like to celebrate regularly the great things God has done. The book you hold in your hands is proof. It's simply a party on paper dedicated to thanking and praising God for His gifts to us in this mission.

As we explore God's gifts to us, we begin to realize that everything we do and everything we are in Young Life is a gift from beginning to end: the privilege of searching for lost kids; the thrill of finding kids with the love of God; and the joy of watching kids grow. "From the fullness of his grace we have all received one blessing after another" (John 1:16). That's the kind of compounding joy you'll discover in *Collecting Lost Coins: 21 Days of Celebration with Young Life.*

You may recognize some of these stories. We've extracted them from a variety of Young Life sources: letters from the President's Office, articles in Young Life publications and some fresh from our friends in the field. Donna Hatasaki, an experienced writer and one of my assistants, has taken each story and created a centerpiece of celebration that compels us to thank God for the great work He has done. I enjoy her style, and I think you will as well.

Another great author, Henri Nouwen, once said that there are two kinds of people in this world, those who are resentful and those who are grateful. This book will help you strengthen your "grats" — those muscles we exercise to become grateful people who praise God. I hope you enjoy the daily discipline of celebration in *Collecting Lost Coins*.

Denny Rydberg
Young Life President

Welcome to the Party!

Or suppose a woman has ten silver coins and loses one. Does she not light a lamp, sweep the house and search carefully until she finds it? And when she finds it, she calls her friends and neighbors together and says, 'Rejoice with me; I have found my lost coin.' In the same way, I tell you, there is rejoicing in the presence of the angels of God over one sinner who repents.

— Luke 15:8-10

*M*ark Lo walked down the West Coast sidewalk, trying not to look lost. It's not that he didn't know his way home. He was painfully familiar with the concrete maze he maneuvered daily from the city bus stop to his parents' apartment a few blocks away. Mark certainly knew the way home, but he was feeling lost just the same. And he was trying his 16-year-old best not to show it. He had skillfully mastered the look of the moment — the shoes, the jewelry, the confident strut. And his bulky sweatshirt gave at least the illusion that there were menacing muscles hiding on what was an otherwise slight sophomore frame. Mark had even shaved his school's initials into the back of his hair in a dramatic declaration that he did belong somewhere — to something.

But as Mark clipped the last street corner and locked eyes on the front door of his parents' apartment, he was once again confronted with the conviction that he simply didn't belong. Mark's parents were not only from some ancient generation across the years, they were from an ancient culture across the sea. Not only did they speak "old-people-ese," they spoke Chinese. Not only did they struggle to understand American culture, but American adolescent culture was out of the question. Mark didn't believe he belonged in his parents' world, and he doubted he belonged in their home. At night he slept on the sofa because they rented out his bedroom for extra income.

Late at night, after everyone else was asleep, Mark would often stare at the living room ceiling and dream of becoming a police officer. Then he would have the power and the respect he craved. Then he would matter to someone. Surely then he wouldn't feel like a coin lost in the sofa anymore.

Later that year, Mark met a Young Life leader on his high school campus. This leader seemed different than most adults Mark had known. For starters, he seemed very glad to meet Mark. He struck up a conversation and treated Mark as if he had hidden value. The leader had the look of a wild-eyed explorer on the verge of some great discovery. And he kept coming back to school. Week after week, the leader swept across the campus in search of kids like Mark. One day, after many conversations, back slaps and smiles, the leader made Mark an offer. "Take a trip with me," he said. "I want you to go to Young Life camp. It will be the best week of your life."

At camp, Mark heard the truth about Jesus Christ. At first he found it hard to believe that God would lower Himself to our level to search for us and would freely lose His life in the process. But then Mark considered the many trips his leader had made to campus. He recounted the many conversations and the warm light in his leader's eyes. Gradually that same light ushered the dawn of a new idea into Mark's mind. Maybe he was the object of an eternal treasure hunt. Maybe he did have hidden value, undiscovered by the world. Maybe Jesus would set aside the wealth of heaven to dig in the sofa for one lost coin.

We have real reason to celebrate in Young Life. We've been entrusted with an eternal treasure hunt and given the great privilege of collecting lost coins! And every year,

thousands of kids like Mark are swept up in the search!
Certainly our work is never done, and it often comes at
a real price of personal sacrifice and sometimes pain. We
light our lamps with the love of God; we sweep the house
and empty our lives of power, position and privilege;
and we never stop searching for lost kids. But Christ
makes something perfectly clear in Luke 15. He expects
us to party along the way! We've been invited — maybe
even instructed — to call our friends and neighbors and
celebrate with the angels every time we collect a lost coin.

On the following pages, you'll find 21 reasons to
celebrate with Young Life. Not only are we celebrating the
lost coins we've collected, but we're celebrating the process
from beginning to end.

In "Celebrating the Search," we marvel at the mystery
of the incarnation and the privilege Young Life leaders
have of becoming Jesus Christ to kids again today. In
"Celebrating the Find," we praise God for the diverse
collection of lost coins who have been recovered by
the Savior through Young Life. And in "Celebrating
the Shine," we bask in the reflected glory of God in
kids as they begin to follow Jesus for the first time. The
transformation is clear. As kids rub up against the character
of Christ, coins who have been previously covered with
corrosion begin to reveal the imprint of the King. Each
day of celebration will include Scripture for reflection,
a colorful Young Life story, a brief prayer and a couple
questions to consider and discuss. We hope you will enjoy!

Friends and neighbors, it's time to put on your party

hats! Let's praise God for the countless kids like Mark whom Jesus Christ has found! And let's celebrate the search as well as the shine! Welcome to the party in Young Life!

The Search

In "Celebrating the Search," we marvel at the mystery of the incarnation and the privilege Young Life leaders have of becoming Jesus Christ to kids again today.

the search

Day 1

In Young Life, the high school cafeteria comes close to sacred ground. For more than 60 years, it has been a key place of contact between Christ and kids through the flesh and bone of Young Life leaders who drop in for a visit at lunch.

On April 20, 1999, however, that sacred ground became a battleground when hundreds of kids hit the cafeteria floor at Columbine High School in Littleton, Colo. Among the faces pressed against the cold concrete that morning was Young Life Area Director Kevin Parker.

Kevin was on campus to grab a friend for lunch when a janitor ran through the room screaming, "Down! Down! Down!" According to Kevin, the next three minutes were "the most intense and fearful" moments of his life. There were gunshots and pipe bombs, and then a mass exit of students and adults from the building. Kevin escaped unharmed. Sadly, 15 others didn't. Fourteen students and one teacher lost their lives that day at school.

That night, Kevin and Kerry Parker's home was flooded with hurting kids. Several Young Life staff members from around the state were already on hand to help steady kids as the first waves of grief began to crash against the community. In some respects, it seemed God had been bracing Littleton for this tsunami for years. Young Life was 25 years deep in the community and more leaders were connected with kids than ever before. As a result, the ministry served as a sturdy breaker against the storm.

Kids continued to fill the Parkers' home for many nights following the shootings. A common question among the crowd: Where was God that day at Columbine High School?

Not an easy question to answer at such a tragic time. But for kids who came to the Parkers for comfort and consolation, one answer became increasingly clear. Jesus was lying on the cafeteria floor that day as the bullets and bombs exploded. And now Jesus was extending a healing hand through these two faithful friends.

Shortly after the shootings, Kevin wrote these words in a letter, "Young Life leaders will never step into the schools again with the same confidence we once did, but we will continue to be there because our faith compels us to go."

As we celebrate the search in Young Life, we celebrate our God-given compulsion to "go." This compulsion comes clearly from the presence of Jesus Christ in us. The Word became flesh and dwelt among us. He was willing to put Himself in harm's way for the chance to make contact with you and me. And now He presses out from within us to repeat that pattern again and again with kids in the world today. Christ compels us to go to kids with His love. We may face embarrassment, rejection or even bodily harm, but we cannot stay; we must go. And when we go, common ground becomes holy ground — even if it's a battleground — because Jesus Christ makes contact with kids, and the Word becomes flesh once again.

Questions

1. Consider a time when you sensed God making movement toward you. What did that movement look like, and how did you respond?

2. Do you sense Christ compelling you to go to any person in particular with His love today? Are you willing to go?

Prayer

Father,

We are so grateful that it is your nature to get up and go. Thank you that you don't sit and wait.

When you see us, you are compelled to make your way to us with a warm greeting and a kind smile. And when we are hiding, you search for us until you find us and offer us your love. How radically different you are than any god we discover in any other religion of the world.

It is our nature to sit and wait for others to come to us. And it is our nature to run and hide. May your nature continue to uproot our nature and flourish in our lives. May we get up and go to others every day with the love of Jesus Christ.

In His name,
Amen.

You stoop down to make me great.
~ Psalm 18:35c

"Our whole lives are full of rubbish, but now our kids are champions." That was the closing quote from a grateful father in the *People* magazine article profiling a cheerleading coach named Shara Brice.

Shara had purposely planted herself in the Docklands of London, the poorest and most crime-ridden neighborhood of Northern Europe, and set out searching for some kids who wanted to cheer. Cheerleading had been previously unheard of in the region, but two years later, Shara marched an 80-member team through the streets of New York City in Macy's Thanksgiving Day Parade! The Ascension Eagles won more competitions than any other squad in British history at that time, and the community was transformed.

The *People* magazine article was a colorful exposé of encouragement and redemption. In the end, however, the reporter missed an intriguing twist to the cheerful tale. Shara Brice was not simply a cheerleading coach. She was Jesus Christ undercover, stooping down to the Docklands to make a lowly people great.

"You can talk to her about any of your problems," said one Eagle, who seemed to be wise to the secret identity of her friend. "She's like another mum."

Shara, a Young Life leader compelled to go to the poorest part of London with the love of God, helped kids with homework, set high standards for behavior and lifted kids to see life beyond the Docklands. In the process, she created an entire community of "ascension eagles," gave them wings and helped them soar.

As we celebrate the search in Young Life, we celebrate the many faces of the Master in Disguise. He comes as a cheerleading coach, a real estate broker, an algebra teacher and a mom. He slips into kids' lives as a college student, a construction worker, a lawyer and a dad. He wears a million different disguises today, but His mission is always the same. He stoops down to make us great.

We are privileged people in Young Life. Jesus Christ is willing to use our lives as leverage to lift kids, moms, dads and entire communities with the redeeming love of God. In the process, we get a lift as well. He raises each of us above the rubbish and puts us in a parade! May we march through His gates with thanksgiving today. May we enter His courts with praise!

Questions

1. Think of a time when God clearly lifted you with His love. How did He do it, and whom did He use as leverage?

2. Have you ever experienced God using you as leverage for His love in someone else's life? What was required of you in that situation? What was the payoff or the reward?

Prayer

Father,

We've seen it so many times. A kind word lifts a kid's face. A day spent together lifts a kid's spirit. And the realization of your love lifts a kid's life forever.

Thank you for using us as leverage in kids' lives. And thanks for giving our lives a lift at the same time.

We praise you, O God, for stooping down to make us great.

In Jesus' name,
Amen.

> He told them another parable: "The kingdom of heaven
> is like a mustard seed, which a man took and planted in
> his field. Though it is the smallest of all your seeds,
> yet when it grows, it is the largest of garden plants and
> becomes a tree, so that the birds of the air come and
> perch in its branches." – Matthew 13:31,32

*N*orman Rockwell captured the heart of America with his paintings. Who could pick up a copy of the *Saturday Evening Post* without lingering over the cover, longing for the characters to come to life? Rockwell's paintings called out to us to step into the story and complete it. He whetted our appetite with a hint of plot and a touch of conflict, then left our imaginations to run wild. Kind of like Jesus when He told parables. He always left His audience with a clear, colorful picture and a lot of questions to explore.

Maybe that's why Marv Reif learned to paint like Norman Rockwell. Marv loved Jesus, and when he mixed the characters of his life with the colors on his palette, he came up with a parable on canvas that hinted of stories untold. But this accomplished artist wasn't satisfied to simply capture characters on canvas. For more than 30 years, Marv has hung out at Las Lomas High School in Walnut Creek, Calif., hoping to catch the hearts of kids with the love of Jesus Christ. Marv's first rule for reaching kids: be available.

"During basketball season, I go into the gym and just stand there by the bleachers," Marv said. "I watch guys practice and wait for one or two kids to come and talk with me. I still remember DJ," Marv said, recalling a kid from years ago. "DJ was a big guy, about 6 feet 7 inches, and I remember distinctly one day he walked off the court and stuck out his hand. He said, 'I'm DJ. You're Marv Reif. I want to be your friend.'"

Marv's friendship with DJ soon became a lifeline for another young man who was drowning in despair. It was a dark day in December when DJ came desperately looking for Marv.

"I was working on a painting when DJ found me," Marv recalled. "He said, 'You've got to come with me, man. We've got to go see Greg. He's feeling really bad. His girlfriend broke up with him.'" So Marv pulled on his sweats and went with DJ.

"I tell kids, 'For the rest of your life, if you need to talk with me, you can call me up at any time,'" Marv said. "'I'm always available. You can call me up at three in the morning, and I won't care. If you come over and I'm working on a painting, and it's not a good time, I'll tell you and we'll set a time to meet.'"

But that dreary day in December, Marv knew he needed to go. So he pushed aside his painting and headed to Greg's house.

"We got Greg and took him to the school to shoot some

hoops," Marv said. "We played about a three-minute game, and then we stopped. It was rainy, gray, depressing and I could tell Greg's heart and mind were somewhere else. So we went and sat on the stairs outside the gym."

Greg's head was hanging down, so Marv said, "Greg, see those dark clouds up there?" Greg looked up and nodded.

"Behind those clouds, the sun is shining," Marv continued. "And as sure as it is raining, that sun is going to break through."

As if on cue, the clouds parted at that moment just enough to let a shaft of light blind the three basketball players on the stairs. Years later, Marv learned just how dark the day had been for Greg before that moment.

Marv was much older and experiencing his own personal heartbreak when Greg started showing up in his life again as an adult. Greg had met the Lord shortly after that afternoon on the stairs, graduated from high school, played professional baseball for a stint and had since settled down with a wife. When he heard the news that Marv was having a hard time, Greg began visiting his old Young Life leader. The small seed Marv had tossed into Greg's life as a kid had grown into a sprawling tree that now offered shade for a weary friend. One afternoon, Marv was compelled to ask, "Greg, why do you bother? Why do you take an interest in me?"

Greg seemed surprised by the question. "Marv!" he exclaimed. "You saved my life!" Only then did Marv discover the depth of Greg's despair that rainy day in December years ago. The young man had been considering suicide when DJ and Marv came calling at the front door. Today, instead of a tragic memory, Greg is a husband, a father and a leader in his church. Greg's abundant life underscores Marv's second rule for reaching kids: look at each individual with an artist's eye.

"We see a kid, but God sees his wife, his kids, his kids' kids," Marv explained. "Just like with Isaac and Rebekah. They saw two kids in Rebekah's womb, but God saw two nations." We see a mustard seed, God sees a massive plant, and God saved a nation when He saved Greg.

As we celebrate the search in Young Life, we thank God for Young Life leaders who look at kids like they were Norman Rockwell paintings — or mustard seeds — lingering over their lives, searching beneath the surface, expecting layers upon layers of potential to unfold. We thank God for leaders like Marv Reif.

"My ministry is a ministry of availability and a ministry of one. If I just show up and reach one kid, then God can change the world."

Questions

1. Marv's first rule for reaching kids seems so simple: be available. In reality, it can be one of the most difficult things to do. What message is communicated to a young person when an adult drops everything to pay attention?

2. When you were a kid, who looked into your life and saw potential? What difference did that make for you?

Prayer

Father,

Thank you that you have the ultimate artist's eye. You never brush by us in a hurry, but are always available, always interested, always lingering over our lives, ready to step into our story and complete it. Thank you for seeing beneath the surface and letting your imagination run wild. May your dreams for each of us unfold according to your deepest desires.

And may we become more like you. Give us an artist's eye, Father. Teach us to linger over the lives of others, looking for buried treasure, expecting you to show up and change the world.

In the name of Jesus,
Amen.

Consequently, faith comes from hearing the message,
and the message is heard through the word of Christ.
~ Romans 10:17

On Feb. 27, 2003, our country and our culture lost a close friend. Fred Rogers slipped out of our neighborhood that day into his eternal home. An ordained minister, Mr. Rogers left a lasting impression on millions of children over the years. The day he died, one woman told a reporter on the street, "For a long time, I thought God looked like Mr. Rogers."

That's the eulogy we live for in Young Life. Our leaders want to look like Jesus Christ to kids.

Brenda Wallace was one of those leaders. Brenda made friends with kids who were deaf and shared the good news that God loved them. In order to share that good news, Brenda had to learn sign language and break into the deaf culture, a difficult job for a hearing person to do. The day finally came, however, when Brenda knew for certain she was "in." After signing a greeting to a new kid on campus, the kid signed back, "Are you hearing, or are you deaf?" Those were the sweetest words Brenda had ever seen.

To the deaf kids on campus, Brenda looked just like

Jesus. She stepped out of her comfort zone and subjected herself to the limits of their isolated lives. Then she shared the good news in a language that they could understand.

In Young Life, we are committed to communicating God's Word clearly to kids of every kind. When we speak to middle school kids, we use concrete examples and limit ourselves to less than 10 minutes for a club talk. When we talk to high school kids, we take more time and introduce abstract ideas. When we speak to kids who can't hear, we use sign language and include interpreters on stage at camp. We have some clubs where Spanish is spoken, and some clubs where club talks are more like simple conversations, because kids are developmentally delayed. And sometimes music is the language that communicates the truth of Jesus Christ most clearly to kids.

Music, however, used to make Shari McMahon sick. Not just irritated and annoyed, but physically ill, like a rough ride on a roller coaster or too many hairpin curves in the back seat of a car. Then Shari went to Young Life camp and encountered special musician Justin McRoberts. Shari later told Justin, "I usually don't like music. I take that back — I hate music. Except for yours. I love the way you deliver the words, how your music sounds, everything."

Not a noteworthy comment, except that Shari McMahon was also deaf. To her unresponsive ears, music was simply rhythmic pockets of air pressure that typically turned her stomach or beat relentlessly against her bones. But Justin's music was different. It swept softly into her silent world and soothed her nauseous soul. Shari told

Justin, "I've decided to accept Jesus Christ because of you."

A few years before he died, Mr. Rogers was interviewed by ABC News about the profound impact his simple message had had on millions of kids. Rogers said he believed that there was a sacred space between the television set and the child who was watching where a "holy enterprise" took place. That sacred space exists in Young Life as well. When leaders stand and deliver God's Word, whether through audible sounds, visible signs or through the mysterious language of music, something holy happens in the space between leaders and kids. In that space, God speaks, ears open and lives are forever transformed.

Questions

1. God speaks to us in many languages throughout our lives. He speaks to us through the beauty of nature, the wonder of a newborn baby, the tragic loss of life. He speaks to us through pastors, friends and parents, the Bible, music and art. When did your heart first hear a word from God? What language did He use, and what did He say?

2. Every week, hundreds of Young Life leaders proclaim God's Word to thousands of kids across

this country and around the world. God promises that His Word will not return to Him without accomplishing everything He had in mind (Isaiah 55:11). Have you seen God's Word at work in the lives of kids recently? What did that work look like?

Prayer

Father,

Thank you for the privilege of proclamation! Thank you for entrusting our tongues and our fingers with the life-giving story of your love. You take our simple words, signs and songs and transform them into something living and active, able to do your work in kids' lives. Thank you! We pray that kids of every kind would have ears to hear the Word of God.

Amen!

Day 5

> We loved you so much that we were delighted to
> share with you not only the gospel of God but our
> lives as well, because you had become so dear to us.
> – 1 Thessalonians 2:8

Studies in education tell us that students remember 90 percent of what they experience but only 10 percent of what they hear.* If that's the case, then statistics are on our side in Young Life. As leaders search for lost kids, not only do they share the truth about Jesus Christ from Scripture, but leaders invite kids to encounter Christ in person by thumbing through the unedited pages of their daily lives. Ricardo was one of those kids.

Ricardo had never met his father. He lived with his mother and his half-brother in a one-bedroom apartment on the rough edge of an impoverished area nicknamed "Little Mexico." It's tough to be 13 years old, and even more so without a dad. Maybe that's why Ricardo kept running away during his first night at WyldLife club.

The first time Ricardo slipped out of club, his leader found him crouching in the dog kennel outside. Ricardo said he was playing hide-n-seek. The second time he

---

* From *The Cone of Learning,* by Edgar Dale.

disappeared, his leader beat the bushes, searched the kennel and finally found Ricardo on the roof. The next time anyone saw Ricardo, he had his back against the wall and his leader was in his face. "You have to respect people's property, Ricardo," the leader said sternly. "And you have to respect yourself. It's dangerous to climb on the roof. If you do it again, I'm taking you home." Ricardo looked relieved.

The next week, Ricardo's mother called during the middle of club and asked Ricardo to find somewhere to spend the night. She wasn't coming home that evening. It was a tough request for a kid who had just moved to town and had few friends.

After club, the leaders served Oreo cookies to the kids, then Ricardo tagged along home with his leader. When Ricardo got to his leader's house, he asked if he could borrow a baggie. Turns out, Ricardo had stuffed 86 Oreo cookies into the pockets of his pants. His leader looked at him and asked, "Would you like to go to McDonald's?"

At McDonald's Ricardo said, "My mom is a cool mom. She doesn't stay home and clean house like those boring moms. She's an important executive, and she likes to go out and party." The leader just listened, and later wept.

Ricardo quickly became a permanent fixture at his Young Life leader's house and the fifth member of the family. His leader taught him how to say "please" and "thank you," how to throw a baseball and how to behave at the table during dinner. One night, as the family held hands to pray before the meal, Ricardo looked up and asked, "Are you tired of having me at your house 24/7?" Ricardo's leader laughed and said, "You're the second son we've always wanted."

What did Ricardo learn about Jesus Christ his first year in WyldLife? Not much from the club talks. He was too distracted. But he learned a lot from his leader's life. He learned that Jesus is the good shepherd who goes and gets His lost sheep — out of the dog kennel, off of the roof — then gives His sheep clear boundaries to keep them safe. He learned that Jesus feeds His little lambs (hamburgers and Oreos) and gives them the time and attention they desperately need. And Ricardo learned that the Father welcomes him at His table 24/7. He's glad to have Ricardo as His "second son."

That was four years ago. Today, Ricardo is a junior in high school and a dedicated catcher on the baseball team. He says "please" and "thank you" without prompting, and he clears his dishes from the table like a pro. And Ricardo loves Jesus. The Jesus he reads about in Scripture, and the Jesus he first encountered, thumbing through the dog-eared pages of his leader's open life.

Questions

1.   We typically think of hospitality as the act of opening our homes and making someone else

feel warm and welcome. But possessing a spirit of hospitality doesn't require that we own a home. Hospitality is an attitude that says, "Welcome into my life. I'm so glad you're here." Think of someone who exudes this spirit. What characteristics of this person quickly come to mind?

2. Hospitality has been a hallmark of Young Life since the first days of this mission. We share our lives as well as our words. What are the unique challenges that come with this kind of ministry? What are the rewards?

Prayer

Father,

Thank you for giving us more than words on a page. Thank you that the Word became flesh and made His home among us. Then He invited us into His life and called us friends.

May the warm welcome of Jesus saturate our souls, Father. And may we become His warm welcome in the lives of lost and lonely kids.

In the generous spirit of our friend Jesus, Amen.

For the word of God is living and active. Sharper than any double-edged sword, it penetrates even to dividing soul and spirit, joints and marrow; it judges the thoughts and attitudes of the heart. – Hebrews 4:12

On paper, a typical Young Life club looks like the most ordinary list of activities: a few songs, a funny skit, a short talk about Jesus. In reality, club is a crossroads where heaven and earth collide. Thirty years ago, a young girl named Mary experienced a collision at that crossroads that changed the course of her life.

Mary only went to one Young Life club in high school. It was the end of her senior year. She was on the fast track to marry her high school sweetheart, and she stopped by club simply to kick up the dust with some friends. By the end of the evening, however, it was the dust of destiny that seemed to be spinning in the air around Mary. Today, she recalls that club clearly.

"Stepping into that room was like stepping out of a black and white world into a world of living color," she said. "There was a warm spirit of hospitality, a lot of laughter and a ridiculous skit. We sang, 'It only takes a spark, to get a fire going …' and 'Country roads, take me home …' Singing had never seemed like so much fun."

After the songs and the skit, the room settled into a vibrant silence as kids listened to the leader up front talk about Jesus. Mary leaned forward to listen and was hanging on every word when suddenly a question rang out from the silence within her soul. "How would you like to be married to a man like the leader up front?"

The question cut through Mary's heart like a burning blade. Where did it come from, that question? Who would dare raise it? The only men Mary had known in her life were nothing like the leader up front. Her father was an alcoholic, and her boyfriend was abusive. Who was she to expect anything more from a man than pain?

Still, the question had made its mark in Mary and now she would never be the same. So in an unexpected act of faith that disappointed both her friends and her family, Mary went home, broke up with her boyfriend and started praying every day for God to send her a man like the leader up front at club. Five years later, Mary had her second-ever contact with Young Life when she met Mark. Mark was on Young Life staff, and it wasn't long until Mary knew he was the answer to the question that had cut through her heart at club.

Mary only went to one Young Life club in high school, but she has been to about 465 since. Mary is a volunteer leader, married to Mark, and together they work hard every week to create a crossroads for kids where heaven and earth collide.

As we celebrate the search in Young Life, we thank

God for the surprising privilege of club — surprising because it's so simple, a privilege because it's profound. With club, we create a space in kids' lives where God is free to speak and act. Sometimes He simply asks a question, and kids are never the same.

Questions

1. Jesus often created a crossroads for people by asking a question. He asked a blind beggar, "What do you want me to do for you?" He asked the disciples, "Who do you say that I am?" He asked an invalid of 38 years, "Do you want to get well?" Has God ever asked you a question that created a crossroads in your life? What was the question, how did He pose it and how did you respond?

2. Henri Nouwen defined a "spiritual discipline" as a tool that we use to create space in our lives in which God can speak and act. According to that definition, Young Life club qualifies as a spiritual discipline for kids! What tools do you use in your own life to create space for God to speak and act?

Prayer

Father,

It is mind-boggling to consider all that you've accomplished in more than 60 years of Young Life clubs. The questions that you have raised with kids, the truth that has taken root and transformed lives.

Thank you for the privilege of participating in this profound process. Thank you for taking our simple songs, skits and talks and creating a crossroads where heaven and earth collide. Thanks most of all for showing up every week ready to speak and act.

We stand amazed and grateful, Father. May we be ever mindful of your holy work in club.

In your name,
Amen.

What is more, I consider everything a loss
compared to the surpassing greatness of knowing
Christ Jesus my Lord. — Philippians 3:8a

It was the worst week of his life. His name was Jim, but after hearing some of his story, you might call him "Job." Jim was a high school kid at a Young Life winter camp that started out bad and systematically went to worse. But like his counterpart from the Old Testament, Jim came face to face with his Creator at the end of his ordeal, and suddenly everything looked different. Here is the chronology of events:

> **Day One:** Jim gets sick on the bus ride to camp and throws up in front of all his friends.

> **Day Two:** Jim falls down on the ski slope and breaks his glasses. Now he's as blind as a bat.

> **Day Three:** Jim slips on the ice as he is climbing into the hot tub at camp and cuts his knee. His leader takes him into town for stitches. On the ride back to camp, Jim props his leg on the dashboard, and his foot freezes to the windshield.

Day Four: Jim meets Jesus Christ and declares, "This has been the best week of my life."

In Young Life, we have access to some of the most pristine property in the world. We are known as experts in camping, offering excellent facilities, dynamic activities, the finest meals, the best music, world-class speakers and the warmest staff. Yet, as we celebrate the search in Young Life, we thank God that it's not our properties or our programs that transform kids. Even the worst week of a kid's life can become the best week, if he or she meets Jesus Christ.

Now back to Jim's story — or was it Job's?

If you recall, Job had three friends, a troublesome trio to say the least. Once Job met his Creator face to face, God put it on Job to pray. Job 42:10 says, "And the Lord restored the fortunes of Job, when he prayed for his friends, and the Lord increased all that Job had twofold."

Jim had a few friends, as well. In fact, he made a list of 12 and started praying with his Young Life leader that his friends would meet Christ. The following summer, the whole lot joined Jim and his leader at Young Life camp and decided to follow Jesus. In one week, God increased Jim's fortune at least twelve-fold.

Fifteen years later, one of those friends wrote his leader to say "thanks." He had just returned from overseas where he had helped train foreign missionaries to share Jesus. Here is some of what he said:

"For 16 days I had the attention of several hundred missionaries in Chiang Mai, Thailand; Myanmar,

Cambodia; Vietnam and Laos. What I taught them will benefit many, many people throughout Asia." Fifteen years after his initial investment in prayer, Jim is one of the richest men in America, if not the world.

As we celebrate the search in Young Life, we thank God that even the worst week of a kid's life can become the best week if he or she meets Jesus Christ. And we thank God for kids who join us in the search, praying fervently for their friends and collecting a compounding fortune in lost coins.

Questions

1. Can you think of a time in your life when the worst day, worst week, worst experience was transformed into something wonderful by a personal encounter with Jesus? Are there any possessions, priorities, plans or dreams in your life that have faded in importance compared to the surpassing greatness of knowing Christ?

2. In Matthew 7:7-8, Jesus encourages us to ask, seek and knock in prayer, because our Father is ready to rise in response. Have you seen Him rise in response to a request from you recently? Share the story.

Prayer

Father,

You wait on the edge of your throne, ready to rise and respond to our requests. Apparently, you've been up and out of your seat a lot in the past 60 years in Young Life.

A small group of ladies in Mrs. Frasher's living room prayed for the kids at Gainesville High School in Texas, and you got up and sent Jim Rayburn.

A couple of Campaigner kids prayed on the side of a mountain in Colorado, and you got up and gave us Frontier Ranch.

A grateful kid 15 years ago asked for his friends to meet Jesus. You were up in an instant and today missionaries in Asia are still feeling the effects of your response.

Thank you, Father. Your generous answers make us want to ask for more!

There are millions of kids who do not know you. We ask that each one would come face to face with the surpassing greatness of knowing Jesus. We ask for warriors who will pray, stewards who will give, leaders who will go and a kingdom that will come as a result.

We know this is not too much to ask. Our Father can do all things.

Amen!

The Find

In "Celebrating the Find," we praise God
for the diverse collection of lost coins
who have been recovered by the Savior
through Young Life.

the find

Day 8

Therefore, since we are surrounded by such a great
cloud of witnesses, let us throw off everything that
hinders us, and the sin that so easily entangles, and let
us run with perseverance the race marked out for us.
— Hebrews 12:1

In the heart of New York City lies a flat piece of concrete boxed in by metal fences called "The Cage." The Cage is a street-league basketball court where common kids get to mix it up with the uncommon talent of NBA and college stars in the sweltering heat of a city summer. Basketball fans come from across the country with hopes of spotting a big name or landing a lucky spot in a three-on-three pick-up game in The Cage. This city court has become such a prime piece of property that it's featured in a popular video game for kids.

Meanwhile, some 400 miles south of New York City lies another important piece of concrete called "The Slab." Like The Cage, The Slab is an outdoor basketball court located in rural Giles County, Va. Besides a catchy name and similar dimensions, however, the two courts have nothing in common. The backboards at The Slab are broken and the rims are bent at 45-degree angles with no nets. Weeds grow from the cracks that create a 4-inch drop-off at about half court. And kids don't come here looking to play basketball. They come here looking for friends, looking for love, looking for real life.

Likewise, you won't find any NBA talent on this crumbling court, but you will find some uncommon college students mixing it up with kids. Not basketball players, but Young Life leaders. Not out to make a name for themselves, but out to love kids for Jesus Christ.

One "season" at The Slab, two Young Life leaders challenged three brothers to a pick-up game of sorts. The two leaders traveled 25 miles from Virginia Tech to the court twice a week, just to spend time with the boys on their territory. Somewhere mid-season, the boys began to pick up on the idea that these leaders offered exactly what they wanted. By season's end, two of the three brothers decided to follow Jesus.

The race marked out for us in Young Life includes country roads as well as city streets. And waiting at the end of those long, rural roads are small groups of great kids looking for love and real life. We thank God for those kids and for the leaders who have the rugged endurance to travel hundreds of miles to find them.

No one travels across the country to see The Slab. But a great cloud of witnesses gathers around that important piece of property with wide-eyed anticipation any time kids appear. And when a Young Life leader steps onto the court, you can bet the crowd goes wild.

Questions

1. How do you think kids in rural America might differ from kids in the suburbs or the cities? How might they be the same?

2. When you consider the race marked out for you, what scenery surrounds your path? Do you sense God calling you to serve a particular group of people in a particular setting?

Prayer

Father,

Thank you for the passion you have for kids of every kind. We thank you in particular for the great kids who live in rural America. In the cheering cloud of witnesses, you are their biggest fan.

Father, we pray for Young Life leaders who search the countryside for lost kids. Give them good cars and lots of tread on their tires. And give them frequent flashes of your face, cheering in the crowd. May your passion possess us all, and give us perseverance for the race.

In the name of Jesus,
Amen.

Day 9

the find

He rescues and he saves; he performs signs and wonders
in the heavens and on the earth.

~ Daniel 6:27

"Our family was a sinking ship until we found the Lord through Young Life," Jan Kraska told the attentive crowd at the Young Life banquet. Jan was the competent captain of the ship, a successful dentist who lived with his wife, Shelley, and three kids in a two-story brick home in Greensboro, N.C. Beneath the smooth surface of their suburban lives, however, there were splintered holes in the family's hull, and the Kraskas were taking on water at an alarming rate.

By high school, middle child Ryan had been arrested three times and was swimming in the swirling waters of drug abuse and delinquency. Oldest child Chad was diving headfirst into the party scene at school. Youngest child Lucy was sinking into a dark pool of depression, and Shelley was long dragged down by the undertow of addiction that seemed to be swallowing her family whole. Meanwhile, Jan just went to work.

"I was pursuing happiness through being a successful

dentist but was really pretty empty," Jan said. "I didn't have a lot to give."

Often in a search and rescue operation at sea, it's difficult to recall the exact chain of events. There are winds and waves, arms and legs, ropes and ladders and hopefully, in the end, an exhausted group of grateful people huddled together in warm blankets, just glad to be alive. That's the case with the Kraska family. It's hard to say what happened when. It's clear that Chad was rescued first and Lucy last, and it all took place within a decade. But the rest is ropes and ladders and Young Life leaders, moving in and out of the stormy scenes of the Kraskas' broken lives.

- Shelley was rescued by two retired Young Life leaders, Barb Lipe and Diane Wise, who invited her to a Bible study shortly after she was released from an alcohol abuse treatment program. "I was the only one coming for a whole year," Shelley said. "But the leaders kept having it because I was coming."

- Chad and Ryan were pulled to safety by the persistence of Area Director Bill Goans, who pursued the boys against all odds. "Bill loved those guys when he had every reason to give up on them," Jan said. "He was rejected 500 times."

- Lucy needed a sign to show her the way to shore, so God provided two Young Life leaders and a flock of geese. "I had just gotten out of the hospital for being depressed and suicidal," Lucy said. "My parents were going out of town and asked leaders Ashley and Bill McCarthy to stay with us. I take forever to warm up to somebody. But one night we were driving to get dinner when Bill stopped the car in the middle of the street. To the right was a big field of geese. He and Ashley jumped out and ran through this field chasing geese. I just sat and watched them. They were the coolest people I'd ever met. Ashley was the one who led me to the Lord," Lucy said. "She loved me like I'd never been loved before."

- As for the captain of the ship, Jan surrendered to Jesus at a Young Life adult weekend camp during the simple act of worship, singing songs. "It was so emotional for me. I found myself crying, really wanting to sing to the Lord."

As we celebrate the find in Young Life, we thank God for the transformation that's taking place in the suburbs. Though families may continue to capsize, we have real reason to hope. The Kraska family serves as a clear case in point. Shelley eventually became an active member of the local Young Life committee. Lucy became a Young Life leader. Chad went to seminary, and Ryan studied to become a dentist like his dad. To be a dentist like his dad, however, Ryan had to focus on prayer more than performance, and service more than success.

"I pray with my employees at the beginning of each day," Jan said. "The office is not about business. It's about serving people."

We have real reason to hope in Young Life. Jesus still rescues and saves and performs signs and wonders in the heavens and on the earth.

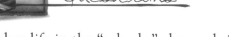

Questions

1. How has life in the "suburbs" changed since you were a kid? Since your parents were kids?

2. Do you know of a family who is taking on water right now and in need of a rescue by Jesus? What might this family look like if each member were transformed? Imagine the father praying with employees at work. Imagine the mother serving Christ and the kids attending seminary or reaching others. Imagine what signs and wonders God might perform. Is God asking you to play a part in the rescue? If so, what is He asking you to do?

Prayer

Father,

Thank you for the search and rescue teams you've stationed in the suburbs, ready to dive into swirling waters in the name of Jesus Christ. May you give those "first responders" strength for the mission and an increased awareness of the signs and wonders you perform.

Save our families, Father. We are battered and broken and need your help. Thank you for hearing our S.O.S.

Amen.

the find

Day 10

From the fullness of his grace we have all received
one blessing after another. For the law was given
through Moses; grace and truth came through
Jesus Christ. ~ John 1:16,17

The newspaper article quoted a social services expert regarding kids who cause trouble in society. The expert said that the secret to correcting these teens was "matching the right program with the right kid." That might be the case. Correcting kids might be a matter of finding the right program, but recreating kids is a matter of finding the right person.

It was the first night of summer camp, and a group of tough kids from the city had hardly unpacked when the leaders received word about a theft. A work crew kid was missing a wallet, $35 and a watch. The next morning, Kirk Davis, the staff person from the city, found the empty wallet in his cabin. He immediately called his guys together and hit them with the hard facts.

"Man, you guys did exactly what society expected you to do," Kirk said, pointedly. "You just proved them right. And it's a shame. Now you've got 20 minutes to produce that money and the watch, or we're all going home."

Kirk walked out and shut the door. He could hear the guys shouting at one another and scrambling around inside the cabin. In a moment, the door opened again and the toughest kid in the crowd presented Kirk with the $35 and the watch. The stolen money was already spent, but the kids had emptied their pockets and pooled their cash.

When the work crew boss came to pick up the stolen goods, he asked, "Who did it?" Kirk replied, "We all did it. We're all guilty. We're in this together." The kids were shocked by Kirk's claim. Then he shut the door and started to preach.

"Let's talk about grace," he said to the silent cabin. "Grace is getting something you don't deserve. God is going to correct you, but He's also going to forgive you. Jesus is going to break you, but He's going to remake you. We all deserve to go home, but we're going to get to stay." It was only the first morning of camp, but God already had the undivided attention of 17 tough guys from the city.

A few nights later, Kirk invited the work crew kid who had been robbed to come to his cabin and to share his own experience of God's grace with the guys. After the young man left that night, Kirk said, "Now I'm going to say a prayer, and if any of you want to pray with me and give your lives to Jesus Christ, then just do it."

Correcting kids might require the right program, but recreating kids requires the right person. That night, 17 broken boys were recreated by Jesus Christ.

Questions

1. What role did "the Law" play in bringing the boys in the story to Jesus? What role has the Law played in your own journey with the Lord?

2. Think of a time when you got something good that you didn't deserve. What effect did this grace have in your life?

Prayer

Father,

Thank you for giving us the great privilege of loving kids from urban settings. We see beyond the razor wire that surrounds their guarded hearts. We see your broken image, isolated and alone. And we long to see that image come to life.

Thank you for reaching beyond the razor wire with grace and truth. Thank you for recreating kids from the city with your love.

We thank you for leaders like Kirk, Father. Protect them, strengthen them, give them your eyes, your ears, your words. Remind them that the Right Person is always with them, offering everything they need.

In the name of Jesus,
Amen.

the find

Day 11

[Love] always protects, always trusts, always hopes, always
perseveres. Love never fails. — 1 Corinthians 13:7,8a

Frodo Baggins may seem like an unlikely character to teach us about teen moms. He's a hobbit, after all. Still, his fictitious life lends us a story we can look to for instruction as we seek to minister to teen moms today.

The central character in J.R.R. Tolkien's *Lord of the Rings* is on a difficult journey with his friends. Responsibility has been thrust upon him, and the carefree days of childhood snatched away like a dream at dawn. Then comes the crucial moment — at least in the movie — when Frodo climbs into a boat and leaves his companions on the shore behind. Except for one headstrong hobbit. Faithful Sam Gamgee jumps into the water to follow Frodo.

Frodo rebukes his friend and says, "Sam, I'm going to Mordor, and I'm going alone." Soaking wet, Sam climbs into the boat and stubbornly replies, "Of course you are, Mr. Frodo. And I'm going with you."

So it is with Young Life staff and volunteers who mentor teen moms. Since the early 1990s, these faithful friends have climbed into the boat with young girls who face the difficult journey of giving birth and raising a child. Of course, the girls face some parts of the journey absolutely alone. And, of course, the stubborn adult leaders are determined to go with them through it all.

"There is a critical window of time when the girls are pregnant or have just had the baby that can determine the path they take from that point forward," said Betsy Stretar, the first missionwide director of Young*Lives*, Young Life's ministry to teenage moms. "Young Life leaders who can really show the love of Christ and walk with them during that difficult time can really influence the course of their lives."

Ashley Nickel would have to agree. Ashley was an unwed mother at 17, living with her boyfriend in Visalia, Calif., when Mary Somerville, the founder of the ministry that would become Young*Lives*, matched her with a mentor who made the difference.

Mary explained, "Sue Hayslett was in her 60s when I asked her to mentor Ashley. Sue said, 'What in the world do I have in common with this girl?' I told her, 'You have love, and that's exactly what she needs. Ashley's mother died when she was 3 years old, and her father was an alcoholic. Love from a 60-year-old will do just fine.'" So Sue jumped into the water to follow Ashley through her pregnancy — her first one and her second.

"Sue took it like a trooper," Mary said. Or maybe like a headstrong hobbit.

Eventually the stubborn love of Jesus Christ set Ashley's life on a new course. Ashley and her boyfriend,

Erik, decided to follow Jesus and were married in Sue's back yard. Today, Erik pastors a church and Ashley recruits women to mentor teenage moms.

Teen moms face a difficult journey, but love always perseveres. As we celebrate the find in Young Life, we thank God for leaders and mentors who gladly get in the boat with teenage moms and paddle tirelessly through a current that can change the course of their lives.

Questions

1. Imagine for a moment what it must be like to be a teen mom. Your childhood is snatched away like a dream at dawn. You can't hide the consequences of your actions from the world. Shame is your constant companion, yet you face the future alone. That's what it must feel like for many young girls. And that's probably some of what it felt like for the woman caught in adultery in John 8:3. Do you recall how Jesus responded to that woman? What are some words you would use to describe His attitude and actions toward her?

2. Put yourself in Sue Hayslett's place for a moment. What do you think she felt as she first started to

befriend Ashley? When Ashley became pregnant for a second time? When Ashley met Christ, got married and her husband started training to become a pastor?

Prayer

Father,

We cannot cast the first stone, or the second, or any stone at all. Our sins may not be as apparent to the world as some, but they are real, and they cause us to be cut off from you and from the ones we love. Thank you that Jesus was not willing to let us bear the weight of our consequences alone. Thank you that He was determined to go with us, even to the cross where He bore our shame.

Love bears all things. And because He did, we are forgiven and free to go, just like the woman caught in adultery. May we generously share that grace with all the kids who so desperately need it today. And may you send a special grace and kindness to kids who are now teenage moms.

In your name,
Amen.

Day 12

the find

"Which is easier: to say to the paralytic,
'Your sins are forgiven.' or to say, 'Get up,
take your mat and walk'?

"But that you may know that the Son of Man
has authority on earth to forgive sins ..." He
said to the paralytic, "I tell you, get up,
take your mat and go home."

He got up, took his mat and walked out in
full view of them all. This amazed everyone and
they praised God, saying, "We have never seen anything
like this!" — Mark 2:9-12

The Bloom brothers knew a lot about salvage. Duane, Bruce and James Bloom lived in a double-wide trailer in the middle of a junkyard in rural Delta County, Colo. It was a piece of heaven for teenage boys who like to tear things apart and get greasy, with hundreds of cast-off cars and trucks calling out from the front yard, begging to be broken down, parceled out and put to good use. So when the Bloom brothers met Bobby Sepulveda, it was a match made in heaven and a miracle made from car parts by three determined boys.

Bobby was a different kind of castoff at the local high school. Born with cerebral palsy and raised in the middle of a family that was falling apart, Bobby knew very little about salvage. With two brothers in prison for murder and his dad doing time for drugs, it seemed that broken things and people were either locked up behind bars or set aside and ignored. After all, Bobby was serving his own life sentence in a wheelchair, without possibility of parole.

But the Bloom brothers had a plan to break Bobby out of his jail. If they could just get him to Young Life club, surely there he would find freedom. Surely there he would learn something about salvage.

Unfortunately, Delta was one of the poorest counties in Colorado with a shortage of social services for kids with special needs — needs like a van with a wheelchair lift to transport Bobby and his 300-pound chair. But who needs social services when you have three strong boys and a sea of rusting resources lapping daily at your door? With an expert eye, the Bloom brothers carefully selected the privileged piece of metal from their front yard to do the job. With a sturdy hood from an old car and a lot of teenage audacity, the boys built a wheelchair ramp for Bobby. Then they loaded him into the back of Duane's pickup truck and delivered him to club.

By summer, the jailbreak was complete. Bobby was flying through the air on the zip line at camp, racing Ridge Runners around the track and tackling the ropes course, just like any other kid. Sort of. Except that the lifeguards were standing ready to grab Bobby at the end of the zip line. And Area Director Todd Laws was riding shotgun on the Ridge Runner. And it took Bobby's entire cabin to lift him up and over and through the ropes course safely. But Bobby didn't find his freedom in the air or on the track. He found it at the feet of a former policeman. Bill Paige, special assistant to the president of Young Life and former detective from New York City, was the camp speaker that week, and another match made in heaven for Bobby.

"Bill came to Young Life with a police officer's background," Todd said. "And Bobby came [from a family] with a criminal background. At first Bobby said, 'Do I want to listen to this cop?' But as the week unfolded he said, 'I see that I can trust him.'" Bobby also saw that he could trust Jesus. By the end of the week, Bobby had been forgiven and set free.

The dictionary defines salvage as "to rescue from ruin," or "things rescued." So goes the story of the ministry to kids with disabilities in Young Life. Faithful friends with an expert eye see the hidden value in what has been broken and they rescue it from ruin. With limited resources and the audacity of the Bloom brothers, these staff, volunteers and friends keep delivering cast-off kids to Christ. And these kids keep finding forgiveness at His feet. It's a story as old as Mark, chapter two.

In that chapter, four friends tear a hole in a roof and deliver a paralytic to Jesus. When they can't get through the door, they take bold steps to the roof and create a window of opportunity instead. Through that window, we see Jesus in a different light. He's not just the local miracle worker who heals broken bodies. He is the Son of Man with authority on earth to forgive sins. When Jesus has proven His point, Mark says, "This amazed everyone and they praised God, saying, 'We have never seen anything like this!'" And that's what they said in Delta after Bobby met Jesus Christ.

Two days after camp, they started Campaigners, a group for kids and Young Life leaders to discuss how the Bible applies to their lives. The group met weekly at a local café. "Our waitresses knew Bobby's family," Todd said. "They couldn't believe what they saw happening in Bobby's life."

And people on the street couldn't believe what they saw happening on Sunday mornings. Every Sunday morning, Bobby could be seen driving his wheelchair down the sidewalk to church.

Right away, Bobby started inviting his friend, Robert, to join him. The first Sunday that Robert joined Bobby at church, the two went to Todd's house for a barbecue afterward. Before they left Todd's that day, Bobby listened as Robert prayed and gave his life to Christ. The Bloom brothers must have been proud. Bobby had developed an expert eye for salvage.

Questions

1. What moves you most about Bobby's story?

2. God used a discarded car part to get Bobby in front of Jesus. Is there something in your life that you once considered "useless" that God has put to good use?

Prayer

Father,

We don't know why some kids are disabled, but we do know that you use them time and again to give the rest of us a better picture of Jesus. They are a gift to us, and we thank you for the privilege of their presence in Young Life.

Thank you, Father, that you have the original expert eye for salvage. Thank you for reclaiming us from the scrap heap and putting us to good use. Thanks especially for using us to carry kids to Jesus Christ.

Amen.

the find

Day 13

We are fools for Christ ... — 1 Corinthians 4:10a

"It's cool to think that God would send His only Son to die for junior high kids. I mean — we're crazy!"
— *an eighth-grade student from Lynchburg, Va.*

Joe was named chief financial officer of a successful dot-com before the age of 27. But it's not what you could read about Joe in the *Wall Street Journal* that was most impressive. It's what you could read about Joe in an English essay by a seventh-grade student named Kyle.

"The first time I saw Joe, I knew we would be friends," Kyle said. "He smiled at me and shook my hand as if we had been friends forever."

When Joe was not creating Internet companies, he was creating lasting relationships with kids on the early end of adolescence through WyldLife, Young Life's outreach to middle school students. Kyle's essay continued:

"Sometimes, after WyldLife, we go out and get food or to the movies. Joe is teaching me a lot about friendship, and I know I will treasure it forever."

Though there were no stock options or bonus plans in Joe's benefits package as a WyldLife leader, there was a special offer for vacation time that he could never resist.

While his colleagues were lying on a beach in Bermuda or dining on the deck of a cruise ship, Joe spent at least one week each summer taking middle school kids to camp.

"It was fun talking to Joe the whole eight-hour bus ride," Kyle said. "That week, I decided to give my life over to Jesus. Without Joe, I wouldn't have gotten to experience the joy and happiness of God's love."

That was eight years ago. Today, Kyle is a college student, growing in his faith. Meanwhile, Joe never made it out of middle school. Professionally he may have made CFO before he turned 27, but personally he kept passing on promotions that took him beyond the eighth-grade.

Jim Rayburn, the founder of Young Life, said, "There is a season of life when faith flourishes best, and that season is adolescence." Sometimes the soil in kids' lives is most receptive early in that season. As we celebrate the find in Young Life, we thank God for leaders who love middle school kids and introduce them to Jesus Christ. Middle school kids are crazy, after all. Then again, so are WyldLife leaders who pass up promotions and spend personal vacation time riding on a bus for eight hours with kids like Kyle.

Questions

1. What are three words that would have described you when you were in middle school? What was your experience with God at that time in your life?

2. How has life changed for middle school kids since you were in seventh- or eighth-grade? What is the strategic value of reaching kids for Christ at an earlier age today?

Prayer

Father,

For some reason you thought it would be best if we had to gradually grow and develop into adults. The middle school years can be such a tumultuous passage in that process. Bones seem to stretch inches overnight, voices crack and break, emotions run rampant and body odor becomes a favorite topic of conversation among parents of teenage boys. It is a crazy time.

Thank you for giving us the privilege of loving kids at this awkward and uncomfortable age. Thank you for each and every adult whom you have called into the chaos of early adolescence to share the love of Jesus with those precious kids. Some day those kids will be completely developed adults — teachers, surgeons, grocers, lawyers, artists, moms and dads. And they will be deeply grateful for the adults who stood steady in their lives when the upheaval of adolescence turned everything upside down.

Father, in farming, upheaval is necessary for planting crops. The tiller churns the soil and makes it soft and receptive to the seed. Thank you for giving us the opportunity to scatter seed in the soft soil of early adolescence. May your love take root and may Jesus grow and flourish in kids' lives.

In Jesus' name,
Amen.

Day 14

the find

Rejection. The word automatically stirs memories of difficult moments from our childhood. Times when we were picked last, left off an invitation or had our hearts broken. For some kids, however, rejection is more than just an isolated event. It's a way of life.

Take teenagers in Venezuela, for example. Flowing through that impoverished country is a restless river of rejected kids. Sixty percent of the population is younger than 30 years old. A flood of unwanted children is diverged into an eddy of extended relatives and distant friends, and too often empties into the streets.

Leidy and Rosa were two of those kids. Fatherless and abused, the sisters each attempted suicide within a span of six months. In both cases, their mother met them in the hospital with anger, belittled them in front of their friends and promised to punish them for their bad behavior. Shortly after, a friend brought Leidy and Rosa to the Vida Joven house. ("Vida Joven" is Spanish for Young Life.) Vida Joven provided a safe, clean and orderly environment where Leidy and Rosa found acceptance and unconditional love. Through relationships with their leaders, Bible study, club and camp, the sisters were pulled from the swirling waters of rejection and found rest upon the rock of Jesus Christ.

In more than 50 countries around the world, hundreds of Young Life staff and volunteers stand steady in the current, extending a hand of hope to drowning kids. In the summer of 2001, however, for a leader named Andre, the river was real and a young man's life was literally on the line. Gary Parsons, a staff person from Russia, wrote about Andre's heroic response:

> Kids were swimming in a very popular place on the Prut River when a boy slipped into a strong current. When Andre saw him, he immediately dove into the river and grabbed the boy, turned him to the shore and shoved him to safety. After expending his own energy, he himself fell victim to the current and disappeared. His body was recovered three days later.
>
> Our staff in the Ukraine shared that Andre had fasted and prayed before the camp that God would powerfully work in the lives of kids. I think Andre was ready to grab hold of a drowning young boy and turn him to the safety of the shore. I know of no greater story that so parallels our Lord's beautiful act of love.

As we celebrate the find in Young Life, we stand in awe of leaders like Andre. In him we see clearly the heroic heart of Jesus Christ and we are struck with reverent silence in our souls.

Thank you, God, for Andre. And thank you that the silence in our souls will give way to celebration one day soon.

Celebration. The word stirs hope of a party yet to come. A party where countless kids like Leidy and Rosa will enjoy the lavish love of the Father's home forever. A party where leaders like Andre stand decorated in glory, waiting to welcome their brothers and sisters with open arms. And a party where the only river that runs through it flows from the Father's throne.

> *Then the angel showed me the river of the water of life, as clear as crystal, flowing from the throne of God and of the Lamb down the middle of the great street of the city. On each side of the river stood the tree of life, bearing twelve crops of fruit, yielding its fruit every month. And the leaves of the tree are for the healing of the nations. No longer will there be any curse ...*
>
> **— Revelation 22:1-3a**

Thank God for the healing of the nations that is already underway in this world because of the sacrificial love of Jesus Christ. And thank God for the privilege of participating in that process through Young Life.

Questions

1. Imagine what it might be like to be a Young Life leader or staff person in Costa Rica, the Ukraine, Zimbabwe, Germany or Peru. What do you imagine some of the unique challenges might be? Some of the unique rewards?

2. Do you have a story of God's healing work in another country that you can share? What part can you play as an individual in the healing of the nations that is already under way?

Prayer

Father,

We look forward to the day when there will no longer be any curse. No poverty, no rejection, no violence, no death or destruction. Only celebration! Only people from every tribe and nation enjoying your lavish love!

Thank you for the faithful Young Life staff and

volunteers around the world who are sacrificing themselves today in preparation for the party yet to come. Give them everything they need, Father. Encouragement, protection, provision, friends, rest, renewal and the outpouring of your Holy Spirit in kids' lives.

These servants are like the leaves on the tree of life, providing the shade and comfort of Jesus Christ to kids around the world. But leaves on the tree of life are not the same as the living water that is the source of life. May your Spirit continue to flow through our International staff and leaders, making them flourish, making them shine.

Amen.

The Shine

In "Celebrating the Shine," we bask in the
reflected glory of God in kids as they begin
to follow Jesus for the first time. The
transformation is clear. As kids rub
up against the character of Christ, coins
who have been covered with corrosion
begin to reveal the imprint of the King.

the shine

Day 15

You have filled my heart with greater joy than when their
grain and new wine abound. I will lie down and sleep in
peace, for you alone, O Lord, make me dwell in safety.
— Psalm 4:7-8

There are a few things that dads don't typically do. Decorating a daughter's room is one of them. So it was no surprise that Lilly's room was not only badly out of style, but also wildly out of control.

Lilly was in third-grade when her mother abandoned the family, leaving her dad to raise three sons and a daughter on his own. For the next three years, dirt, garbage and clutter collected in Lilly's room, like the pain and chaos that seemed to be collecting around her life. She needed a mother's touch. About that time, a WyldLife leader in Lilly's rural New York neighborhood began looking for the chance to befriend the sixth-grade girl.

"I was looking for a way to step in and be the woman in Lilly's life," Gaye said. "When she and her friend went forward to receive Christ at a concert, I literally ran to be the one to talk with them."

Following the concert, Gaye and the girls decided to

meet weekly for Bible study, but Gaye was prepared to share her life as well as God's Word.

"We went shopping and bought teen Bibles. We went to the Adirondacks and climbed a mountain to do our study. We went swimming and had picnics before our Bible studies. We went to a climbing wall and went tubing and they began to sleep over at my house and bring friends. We grew from three to a group of eight."

One day, the group of girls decided to meet at Lilly's house for the study. That's the day Gaye discovered the depth of despair in the little girl's life.

"You couldn't walk into her room," Gaye said. "The floor was covered, and the room was dirty. There were no sheets on the bed and the mattress was ripped. Privately, I asked her if she would like to fix up her room. Her eyes lit up.

"When we started shopping, she had no opinion about what she wanted to buy, but by the end of the night, she had chosen her colors and decided her style."

Finally it was time for the group of girls to get to work. And work they did. They cleaned, they scrubbed, they soaked six layers of old wall paper with pure vinegar, they scraped, they peeled, they sanded, they buffed and eventually they covered the smooth walls with fresh paint and the bare bed with fresh sheets. It was lavender and lilacs for young Lilly.

"We worked and talked about Jesus washing feet, about having servant attitudes and putting others before ourselves," Gaye explained. "We received blessing after blessing: a used bed, a dresser, a mirror and a clock radio. The girls learned to thank God for supplying all of their needs."

Sometimes the best Bible study smells like vinegar and comes with a can of paint. Sometimes the shine in a kid's life is created with a little love and a lot of scrubbing. And sometimes the glory of God looks like a little girl in a lavender room, buried in a bed of lilacs with a smile.

Questions

1. Has someone in your life served as a second father or mother to you? How has God used them to reveal His love?

2. Can you think of a time when you've seen a kid shine as a result of being lavished with God's love? Tell the story.

Prayer

Father,

Thank you that we get to be part of the process of bringing the luster of your love into kids' lives. Sometimes it takes hard work, Lord, our own money and manual labor. But then we get to see a glimpse of the glimmer and the shine. And there's not a better sight than the glimmer of your glory in kids' lives.

Father, we pray for all the kids who are missing a mother or a father, or maybe both. Remind them that they belong to you, and use our lives to lavish them with your love.

In the name of Jesus,
Amen.

Day 16

Fix these words of mine in your hearts and minds; tie them as symbols on your hands and bind them on your foreheads. Teach them to your children, talking about them when you sit at home and when you walk along the road, when you lie down and when you get up. Write them on the doorframes of your houses and on your gates ...
— Deuteronomy 11:18-20

"Freedom" and "fear" are two terms that are talked about a lot these days, usually in a political sense and on a global scale. But today let's take the debate down to about a size seven. That's the size of a baseball cap worn by a young man named Joseph.

Joseph was a left-handed pitcher on his hometown high school team with a reputation for leaving batters looking foolish at the plate. But when Joseph found himself in a tight spot with runners on base and a big bat on deck, he would take a moment to pause and take off his hat.

Beneath the bill of Joseph's hat was everything he needed to know to face his fears. Scrawled in permanent marker and slightly smeared with sweat were the words, "I can do all things through Christ who gives me strength." Those words gave Joseph the courage to face his fears and the freedom to play his game with focus. And Joseph's game was much bigger than baseball.

When Joseph wasn't throwing curve balls, he was casting nets to draw his friends to Jesus Christ. During his high school years, several of Joseph's friends met the Lord through Young Life because Joseph led the way. He called them every week and invited them to club. He persuaded several of them to go with him to camp. He stood up with his friends at the end of camp when they needed courage to stand before their peers and declare that they had decided to follow Jesus. And when they got back home, Joseph rounded up his friends and took them with him to church.

Kids today live in a world where fear threatens freedom on a global scale. Now more than ever, kids need the Word of God tucked tightly in their caps. As we celebrate the shine in Young Life, we thank God for leaders who help kids learn and memorize God's Word. God's Word gives kids the courage to face down their fears with faith, and the freedom to share Jesus with their friends. May we tie it on our hands, bind it on our foreheads, mark it on our baseball caps and continue to teach God's Word clearly to kids as long as we exist in Young Life.

Questions

1. Is there a fear that you need to face down today? What word from God do you need to tuck beneath your cap for courage?

2. In Young Life, we are committed to integrating kids into a local church congregation when they decide to follow Jesus Christ. What are some of the challenges we might face in this process? Can you think of some suggestions or solutions that could help us succeed?

Prayer

Father,

Your word is living and active and sharper than a double-edged sword. There is really nothing else like it in our experience. It instructs us, rebukes us, corrects us, encourages us and gives us strength to live. May we memorize it, meditate on it and turn it loose in our lives. And may we turn it loose daily in the lives of kids.

In the name of Jesus,
Amen.

Day 17

And surely I am with you always, to the very end of the age. – Matthew 28:20b

atalie Gilbert will likely never forget Friday, April 25, 2003. That's the day the 13-year-old girl stood center court at a Portland Trail Blazers game singing the solo of a lifetime. Halfway through the national anthem, however, before a packed crowd and television audience, Natalie forgot the words. On the verge of tears, Natalie looked desperate. That's when Blazers Coach Maurice Cheeks made his move. Maurice met Natalie at center court, put his arm around her and started to sing. Soon the whole arena joined the chorus. What could have been one of the darkest moments of Natalie's life, *USA Today* later named one of the brightest moments in NBA history.

One year earlier, a 12-year-old girl named Allison sat in a hospital bed, facing the solo of a lifetime as well. Allison had just been diagnosed with diabetes, and was facing at least four shots of insulin a day plus numerous finger pricks to check her blood sugar. From an early age, Jesus had trained Allison's heart to sing a tender song of faith, but holding a needle for the first time, she was beginning to forget the words. That's when Allison's WyldLife leader made her move. Dianna Heeb told the doctors that she wanted to give herself shots, too. So the doctors gave Dianna a needle and some saline solution and she practiced injecting herself in the thigh. What could have been one of the darkest moments of Allison's life instead became a moment she would remember with gratitude forever.

Most of us are familiar with a statement from Jesus known as the Great Commission, "Therefore go and make disciples of all nations ..." But underscoring the Great Commission is a line of great compassion. "And surely I am with you always ..." As we celebrate the process of discipleship in Young Life, we thank God for leaders who underscore the Great Commission with great compassion. We thank God for leaders who not only teach and instruct kids to follow Christ, but leaders who join kids center court and help them sing. Those leaders are following in the footsteps of Jesus.

About 2,000 years ago, mankind stood center court looking lost and all alone. We had been accurately diagnosed with a disease that was killing us called sin. That's when Jesus made His move. Our Savior didn't simply watch us from the sidelines, He joined us center court. That's what makes Good Friday "good" and why we sing on Easter Sunday. Jesus joined us in our brokenness and sin and turned death into life, the worst into the best. It was the brightest moment in human history, period. And through Young Life leaders like Dianna Heeb, the light from that moment still penetrates the darkness for kids today.

Questions

1. Can you think of a dark moment in your life that was transformed by the presence of a friend who loved you? Share the story.

2. Make a list of some significant moments in the life of a typical kid today. (The moments could be dark, bright or somewhere in between.) Now imagine a Young Life or WyldLife leader present in each of those moments with that kid. What difference would it make? What role might the leader's presence play in the process of making a disciple?

Prayer

Father,

Thank you that you didn't leave us at center court, lost and all alone. Thank you for stepping into our darkest moment with the bright light of your love. And thank you for giving us the privilege of doing the same for kids today.

Jesus commissioned us to go and make disciples, teaching them to obey everything He commanded us. Thank you that the greatest thing He commanded us to do was love. May we live out that message clearly with kids each day by laying down our lives in Jesus' name.

Amen.

By this all men will know that you are my disciples, if
you love one another. – John 13:35

ohn Lynch knew there was one thing he would never
do. He would never trust Jesus. John grew up with
a father who was both an atheist and a genius and had
skillfully trained his son to guard himself against the follies
of faith. So John's protective walls were perfectly in place
when a group of Campaigner kids came strolling right
through his front door with the love of Christ.

"I was a drama and English teacher at Arcadia High
School in Phoenix," John said. "We cast a play and, what
I didn't know was, two-thirds of the kids were in Young
Life." And what John really didn't know was, those kids
were faithfully praying for him to meet the Lord.

"If adults tried to talk to me about Christ, I wouldn't
listen," John said. "I had all the stereotypes and
preconceptions. But these kids had no pretense, they
had no guile. I would listen to them because I wasn't
threatened. In the end, their love won me to Christ."

John met Jesus on Dec. 23, 1979, sometime after one
of those Campaigner kids asked him to please proofread an
English paper he had written on the resurrection. Defenses

dismantled and his heart warmed by love, John proofread the paper and read the proof that changed his life.

Not long after, John left teaching, went to seminary and eventually became a teaching pastor in Phoenix. But "Playwright Pastor" might be a better title for this man. Besides preaching from the pulpit, John has written plays that portray the love of Christ in terms that a secular audience can understand. One play, *Ask Me Anything*, received five-star reviews and standing ovations at the most prestigious theater in Phoenix. In that play, the lead character develops a mental illness, but meets the Lord through a homeless man who is also mentally ill.

If anyone in the audience happens to be hiding behind walls, the love of Christ comes calling quietly at the front door.

As we celebrate the shine in Young Life, we celebrate the love of Jesus in kids' lives. When kids meet Christ, He shines through them and warms others with His love. In that warmth, protective layers peel away, walls come down, hearts unfold and lives are forever transformed.

 Questions

1. Has God ever used a young person in your life to surprise you with His love? Share the story!

2. Can you recall a time when your reason or logic became a roadblock in your journey with Jesus? Were you eventually able to move forward in faith? Explain the process.

Prayer

Father,

You use the weak to confound the wise. Thank you for the untold times you've used kids to reach adults for Jesus Christ. We've seen more than our fair share of these miracles in Young Life. Thank you!

Today we pray for all the kids we know who have decided to follow Jesus. Guard them, Father, give them your strength and transform them with your presence. Make them a powerful force to be reckoned with on this planet, armed with your disarming love.

In your name,
Amen.

the shine   Day 19

Therefore, if anyone is in Christ, he is a new creation;
the old has gone, the new has come!
~ 2 Corinthians 5:17

ost moms and dads keep a running list of special memories called "Firsts." There was the first time the baby kicked before it was born. The first time mom held the baby in her arms. The first time dad changed a diaper. The first tooth, the first day of school, the first car, the first date. The list can be long and lively, but for Karen Sanders, the list was long and painful from the start. She will never forget the day she first learned that her son, Jake, was born with an extra chromosome and would be defined daily by his special needs.

As the years went by, Jake's needs made him difficult to deal with and sometimes hard to control. Karen's list grew longer with unpleasant memories of difficult phone calls from teachers, parents and bosses complaining about her son. Then came the phone call that stopped Karen's running list right in its well-worn tracks.

Jake's boss called from the grocery store one day to talk about Jake's performance at work. Karen braced herself for another complaint, but then Jake's boss said something that surprised her. Jake's behavior had improved! The boss didn't know how to explain it, but Jake seemed like a new kid. Karen hung up the phone and cried. It was the first time anyone had ever called with a good report about her son.

What had made the difference for Jake? A few months earlier, he had finally met someone who could reach beyond his challenging behavior and tame his troubled heart. Jake went to Young Life camp and met Jesus. Soon after, Jake's mom started making a new list.

There was the first time Jake walked through the door with a Bible. The first time he shared Jesus with a friend. The first time someone called with a good report about this incredible boy. The first time the family joined a church.

When kids begin to follow Jesus Christ, this world becomes a better place. Kids become more productive at school and at work. They gain a sense of self-respect and self-control. Kids who know Christ begin to consider the thoughts and feelings of other people. And families experience the creative power of Christ firsthand.

As we celebrate the shine in Young Life, we thank God for giving kids new lives and for giving parents new lists. Jake Sanders may have a few special needs when it comes to working in this world, but he's not a disabled disciple. Jake is a new creation in Jesus Christ.

Questions

1. Think back to the days when you first started following Jesus. If you were making a list of firsts for those early days, what would be two or three things at the top of the list? "There was the first time I ..."

2. Parents could always use a word of encouragement about their kids. Is there a kid who comes to mind right now in whom you've seen growth or progress in the Lord? Would you be willing to call his or her parents with a good report?

Prayer

Father,

Thank you that you make all things new. This is one of our favorite aspects of who you are. May we never be guilty of pegging other people in a hole, of writing anyone off as a lost cause. Open our eyes to see your creative work in those around us, and open our mouths to share encouragement for what we see.

In the name of Jesus,
Amen.

the shine | Day 20

And may those from the city flourish like vegetation of the earth. – Psalm 72:16b (NASB)

It gets hot in the summertime in the city. You can see the heat rising from the asphalt and feel the pressure rising in people's veins. For kids who have nowhere to go and plenty of time to get there, summer in the city can seem like a sentence in a cell block with no hope for escape.

Bolivar and Armando were two of those kids. Stranded in the heart of south central Los Angeles, the boys were surrounded by heat and pressure with the opportunity for trouble on every side. Until a Young Life leader invited the boys to camp. And some generous adults paid the way so they could go. So instead of standing on street corners, killing time, Bolivar and Armando were swinging through the tops of trees, living life. Instead of staring down rivals in back alleys, they were laughing it up with friends in Young Life club. Instead of listening to the seduction of drug dealers, they were listening to the truth about Jesus Christ. In the middle of the week, Armando told his leader, "I can't be the same, you know. Something's changing in me."

Bolivar and Armando both met Jesus Christ at Young Life camp, but that was just the beginning. In the years that followed, the two friends returned to camp on work crew and summer staff and began serving as WyldLife leaders at home in L.A. With the help of their Young Life leader, the two enrolled in a local college and started living the kind of lives that make a lasting difference in the city. Armando was right. Something had definitely changed.

Across the country, near the Twin Cities in Minnesota and 25 years earlier, a kid named Mike was making money selling drugs and using his profits to support his own addiction. But Mike had another problem. Everywhere he went, he ran into Young Life leaders. They were at the school, at ball games, on the street and anywhere that kids could be found. Mike said, "They were like angels shining in white, and a reminder of God's power and presence. They reminded me, simply by being there, that I was on a road leading nowhere."

Mike finally surrendered to the presence of Jesus in his life. Today, Mike is a pastor and recently told friends at a reunion, "I won't tell you that I'm a pastor today because of Young Life. I'll tell you that I'm alive."

The best hope for urban renewal today is the power of Christ unleashed in the lives of kids like Bolivar and Armando. The best hope for disabling drug dealers is the presence of Jesus unleashed in the lives of kids like Mike. Jesus not only saves souls, He saves lives and grows destructive, drifting boys into powerful men of purpose who change the world.

1. Have you ever experienced the kind of conviction Mike talked about, the conviction that comes simply from the presence of someone who is walking with Jesus when you are not? Tell the story and explain your response.

2. Discipleship in the city sometimes takes on added dimensions because of the obstacles that kids face. Bolivar and Armando's Young Life leader helped enroll them in a local college as part of his commitment to their growth in Jesus Christ. What other steps might leaders have to take in order to help kids follow Jesus in the city?

Prayer

Father,

Thank you for saving the souls of men like Bolivar, Armando and Mike. Thank you also for saving their lives. Today they are powerful men of purpose changing the world. You, O God, can do all things.

We ask for continued transformation in our cities, Father. We ask that you continue to raise up men and women who walk with Jesus down the alleyways and the asphalt, bringing real urban renewal through your love.

Intersect a drug dealer today, Lord Jesus. Send your angels shining in white, or maybe worn-out Young Life T-shirts, to bring the full weight of your glory into this world. May he surrender soon, Lord Jesus. May he surrender to your presence and be saved.

In your name,
Amen.

the shine

Day 21

Where there is no vision, the people perish.
— Proverbs 29:18 (KJV)

In Caren McCormack's scrapbook, there's a photo of Caren as an adult, standing next to Billy Graham during one of his crusades in 1997. Caren was the volunteer director of arrangements and logistics for the crusade where thousands of people came to Christ. Flip back a few pages in her mental scrapbook, however — to the early 1980s in Fort Worth, Texas — and you'll get a distinctly different picture of Caren.

"I was a hurting kid," Caren recalled. "My parents had just divorced. I needed people who would take time with me and listen to me and let me cry and pray for me. My Young Life leader did that."

Through the next two decades, Caren traveled a well-worn path in Young Life. She went to camp, later decided to follow Jesus, served on work crew waiting tables, served on summer staff mowing grass, became a volunteer leader and eventually ended up on committee, serving one of the poorest communities in the country. In between she found time to marry her husband, Jon, start a business, give birth to her daughter, Caroline, and snap a picture with Billy Graham. Caren's photo album is full.

John Trent's photo album is full as well. As an adult, Dr. John Trent has seen his photo on the inside cover of more than a dozen Christian books he has authored or co-authored and in countless brochures describing his international ministry and speaking tours. More importantly, his home is well-decorated with photos of his wife of 23 years, Cindy, and daughters Kari and Laura. Three decades ago, however, John was a hurting kid much like Caren.

Abandoned by his father as a baby, John grew up in a single-parent home in Phoenix, Ariz. Year after year, John waited for his father to come home and take his place in the family portrait. Tragically, his father never showed — but Doug Barram did.

Doug Barram was John's Young Life leader, and Doug showed up at John's football practices, ball games and at school. Doug and his wife invited John and his friends over for spaghetti dinners and simply to hang out.

"I would volunteer to mow their lawn," John said, "just so I could go to their home."

The Barrams gave John a clear picture of Jesus and a vision of what a loving family looked like with a father in the photo. Eventually, John committed his life to Jesus Christ, went to camp and served on work crew. Today, John serves as chairman and CEO of Ministry Insights International, and he credits Doug Barram for making the difference in his life.

"People often forget decades, but they remember moments in their lives," John said. "The pictures we leave other people are powerful. Doug Barram lived that blessing in my life."

As we celebrate the shine in Young Life, we thank God for the powerful pictures in our family album. Pictures of leaders who look like Jesus, standing on the sidelines at football practice, sitting across the table in the cafeteria, waiting in the wings of the theater to say, "Congratulations! Well done!" We thank God for the powerful pictures of leaders leaning forward to listen to kids over coffee or ice cream or big plates of spaghetti, as kids talk and question, get angry, laugh and cry. We thank God for the powerful pictures of leaders sacrificing themselves in service for kids, sharing their lives as well as God's Word and walking with kids through the difficult days and the good. Because, as John Trent and Caren McCormack will tell you, without a vision, the people perish. But with a clear picture of Jesus, people flourish and become whole.

Questions

1. Caren McCormack and John Trent were lost coins as kids. Today they are the eternal treasure of Jesus

and clearly reveal the imprint of a King. Through the love and friendship of Young Life leaders and many others who knew Jesus, God created an incredible scrapbook of amazing moments for both of their lives. In your own life, who has helped give you a vision for who you could become, and how did he or she do it?

2. Think of a young person in your life who might need a vision for the future. What would you like to contribute to that vision? What might you do or say to help create a picture of purpose for this young friend?

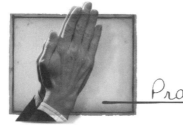

Prayer

Kind and Gracious Father,

How many stories are there of kids like John and Caren? Kids who start with torn and tattered pages of tragic loss and end with a colorful scrapbook of the wonders you have done? So many stories that it will take all of eternity to tell them. All of eternity to thumb through the photos of your amazing love. We look forward to the picture party in heaven that will never end.

Father, we have so much to celebrate because we belong to you! Thank you for giving us the privilege of collecting lost coins! Thank you for the multitude of kids you've collected for your kingdom through Young Life! And thank you for redeeming and restoring each and every one!

In the name of our brother Jesus,
Amen.